A gift for

Eric
_____

From

Willie
_____

Date

5/15/2021
_____

WiseDogs

H. Jackson Brown, Jr. • Dale C. Spartas

WORTHY
PUBLISHING

Brentwood, Tennessee

Photographer's Introduction

Dogs have always been a significant and meaningful part of my life. Often as I work I have a four-legged companion (or two) by my side, or sleeping at my feet, or nudging my hand, telling me "finish up; it's time for play!"

Since boyhood I have been drawn to dogs as they are to me. They grow from chubby, silly, little puppies into attentive, loving companions, and finally into gray-muzzled senior citizens. I've trained many dogs, but the most important lessons learned were the ones I've actually been taught by the wonderful dogs who have passed through my life.

I am blessed and grateful for my family and friends, for my career, for a home on the river, and, of course, for all the wise dogs who have been in my life.

Dale C. Spartas
Big Sky Country, Montana

Author's Introduction

After my Life's Little Instruction Book® series became popular, I searched for a simple way to illustrate instructions from the books.

The answer became obvious when I met Dale Spartas and had the pleasure of viewing his superb photographs of sporting dogs. Something magical seemed to happen when a particular photo was matched with the appropriate instruction. His photographs communicated perfectly the characteristics of loyalty, discipline, purpose, and courage that I had written about.

A quick glimpse of these pages confirms what we already know about our faithful companions; that the mystery behind their eyes and steadfastness of their spirit reveal noble hearts that have much to teach. So relax and let your imagination run free over these words and images. Then go find a dog and pet it.

H. Jackson Brown, Jr.
Oak Hill, Tennessee

Don't live
with the
brakes on.

Take a chance.

The things
around you
are never as
important as
whose arms
are around
you.

If someone
offers you a
breath mint,
take it.

Consequences follow every decision.

Don't skip
breakfast.

Be the first
to say hello.

Resist
temptation.

Don't whine.

Retain
your dignity
regardless of the
circumstances.

Don't
let a little
dispute
injure a great
friendship.

Respect
your elders.

If you're going
to sing,
sing out loud.

When something
is unclear,
don't be afraid
to ask a question.

Practice patience.

Life will
sometimes
hand you
a magical
moment.

Savor it.

Be there
when people
need you.

When
you're wrong,
admit it.

Promise
big.

Deliver
big.

Don't
hurry
past
beauty.

Never
deprive
someone of
hope.

It may be
all they have.

Watch
a sunrise
with someone
you love.

Be the
first to
volunteer.

Win
with humility.

Lose
with dignity.

When you find
a job you love,
give it everything
you've got.

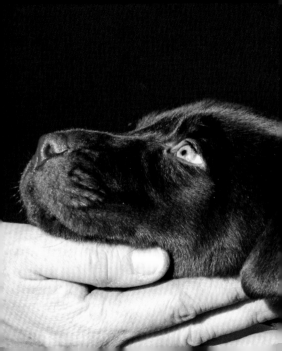

Everyone
needs
a hand to
hold and
a heart to
understand.

Good things
are best
when shared.

Anyone
can have
a bad day.

Waste time
with someone
you love.

Remember,
some things
are worth
waiting for.

Be home
for the holidays.

Never apologize
for being early.

Silence.

Sometimes
it's the best
response.

71

Believe
in love at
first sight.

Let the hard times
make you stronger.

Who you're with is always more important than where you are.

Be the one
who's not
afraid to shake
things up.

Sometimes you'll have to hold your nose, close your eyes, and jump off the high board.

Time alone
is often
time well spent.

Don't go
looking
for trouble.

Remember,
that winners
do what
losers don't
want to do.

Stand by your friends.

Protect and defend
those you love.

May your dreams defy the laws of gravity.

And remember,
your character
is your destiny.